The U.S. Air Force (U.S. Armed Forces)

Matt Doeden
AR B.L.: 2.9
Points: 0.5   MG

The U.S. Armed Forces

The U.S. Air Force

by Matt Doeden

Consultant:
Barbara J. Fox
Reading Specialist
North Carolina State University

Capstone
press

Mankato, Minnesota

Blazers is published by Capstone Press
151 Good Counsel Drive, P.O. Box 669, Mankato, Minnesota 56002
www.capstonepress.com

Library of Congress Cataloging-in-Publication Data
Doeden, Matt.
     The U.S. Air Force / by Matt Doeden
     p. cm.—(Blazers. The U.S. Armed Forces)
     Includes bibliographical references and index.
     Contents: The U.S. Air Force in action—Air Force aircraft—Weapons and
equipment—Air Force jobs.
     ISBN 0-7368-2738-2 (hardcover)
     1. United States. Air Force—Juvenile literature. [1. United States. Air
Force.] I. Title.
UG633.D59 2005
358.4′00973—dc22   2003024299

Editorial Credits
Carrie A. Braulick, editor; Juliette Peters, designer; Jo Miller, photo researcher;
     Eric Kudalis, product planning editor

Photo Credits
AFFTC History Office, 6, 12, 13, 16–17
Capstone Press/Gary Sundermeyer, cover (inset)
Corbis/Patrick Robert, 21(bottom)
DVIC, 19; Ken Hackman, 5; SSgt Karen Z. Silcott, 25; TSgt Derrick Harris, 8–9;
     TSgt Hans H. Deffner, 27; TSgt Jack Braden, cover, 7; U.S. Air Force
     photo/SSgt Grey L. Davis, 28–29
Fotodynamics/Ted Carlson, 22, 23
General Atomics Aeronautical Systems Inc., 15 (bottom)
Getty Images Inc./Paula Bronstein, 26; U.S. Air Force/Tom Reynolds, 20; U.S. Air
     Force photo, 14, 21 (top)
Lockheed Martin Aeronautics Company, 11, 15 (top)

**Capstone Press thanks Raymond L. Puffer, PhD, historian, Edwards Air Force Base
History Office, Edwards, California, for his assistance in preparing this book.**

1 2 3 4 5 6 09 08 07 06 05 04

Table of Contents

★★★★★★★★★★★

The U.S. Air Force in Action

Three U.S. Air Force F-16s soar toward five other jets. The other jets have just entered U.S. airspace.

The U.S. pilots fire several warning shots. The other pilots fire missiles at the F-16s. The U.S. pilots turn and dive to dodge the missiles.

The F-16 pilots fire missiles at the
enemy jets. Two of them explode. The
remaining enemy jets turn around.
The F-16 pilots have won the fight.

BLAZER FACT

The first aircraft used by the U.S. military were hot-air balloons.

Air Force Aircraft

Fighters are the fastest Air Force planes. F/A-22s can fly 1,500 miles (2,414 kilometers) an hour.

F/A-22 fighter

★★★★★★★★★★★★

Bombers destroy targets on the ground. The B-2 Spirit bomber can drop bombs without being seen by enemy radar.

Cargo plane

The Air Force has other planes. Cargo planes carry gear. Stealth planes are hard for enemies to locate. Remote-controlled planes are flown from the ground.

Stealth plane

Remote-controlled plane

F-16 Fighter Diagram

Missiles

Tail

AF
88 **473**

Engine

Missile

★ ★ ★ ★ ★ ★ ★ ★ ★ ★ ★ ★ ★ ★ ★

16

Cockpit

Nose

Weapons and Equipment

Missiles are some of the deadliest weapons of the Air Force. Lasers and cameras guide some missiles to targets.

Bombs destroy targets on the ground. Laser-guided bombs can hit small targets. Bunker busters can destroy underground hideouts.

BLAZER FACT

A JDAM missile takes only 30 seconds to find its target.

JDAM

Oxygen mask

Head-up display

Pilots wear oxygen masks while flying high. Head-up displays show pilots flight information.

Air Force Jobs

Many Air Force members are pilots. Other members fix planes, cook, or keep track of flights.

Air Force members have different ranks. Officers have higher ranks than other members. The Chief of Staff has the highest rank.

BLAZER FACT

Many astronauts were once Air Force pilots.

AIR FORCE RANKS

★ ★ ★ ★ ★ ★ ★ ★ ★ ★ ★ ★ ★ ★ ★ ★ ★ ★

ENLISTED	OFFICERS
Airman	Lieutenant
Sergeant	Captain
	Major
	Colonel
	General
	Chief of Staff

F-16 Fighters

Glossary

airspace (AIR-spays)—the space above a country; a country controls which planes can fly in its airspace.

bunker buster (BUHNGK-ur BUHST-ur)—a large laser-guided bomb built to destroy underground enemy hideouts

dodge (DOJ)—to avoid something by moving quickly

laser (LAY-zur)—a device that makes a powerful beam of light; laser-guided bombs follow laser light to their targets.

radar (RAY-dar)—equipment that uses radio waves to locate and guide objects

rank (RANGK)—an official position or job level

stealth (STELTH)—having the ability to move secretly

Read More

Cooper, Jason. *U.S. Air Force.* U.S. Armed Forces. Chicago: Heinemann, 2003.

Hopkins, Ellen. *U.S. Air Force Fighting Vehicles.* Aircraft. Berkeley Heights, N.J.: Enslow, 2001.

Sievert, Terri. *The U.S. Air Force at War.* On the Front Lines. Mankato, Minn.: Capstone Press, 2002.

Internet Sites

FactHound offers a safe, fun way to find Internet sites related to this book. All of the sites on FactHound have been researched by our staff.

Here's how:

1. Visit *www.facthound.com*
2. Type in this special code **0736827382** for age-appropriate sites. Or enter a search word related to this book for a more general search.
3. Click on the **Fetch It** button.

FactHound will fetch the best sites for you!

Index